ENDURE

Poems by Bei Dao

Translated by

Clayton Eshleman and Lucas Klein

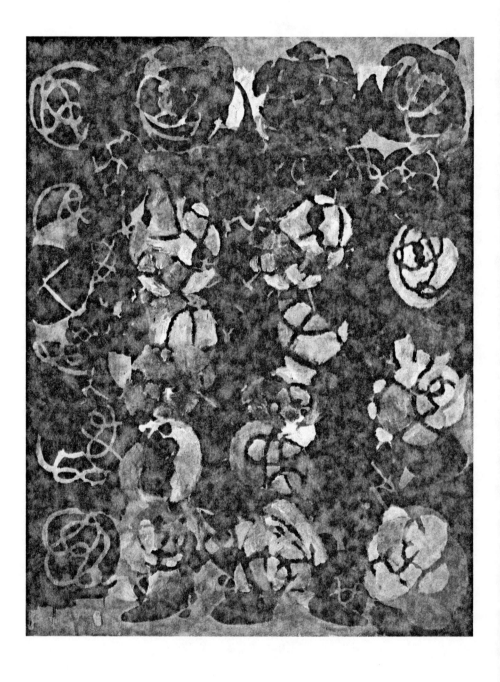

ENDURE

Poems by Bei Dao

Translated by

Clayton Eshleman and Lucas Klein

BLACK
WIDOW
PRESS

Black Widow Press is an imprint of Commonwealth Books, Inc., Boston, MA. Distributed to the trade by NBN (National Book Network) throughout North America, Canada, and the U.K. All Black Widow Press books are printed on acid-free paper, and glued into bindings. Black Widow Press and its logo are registered trademarks of Commonwealth Books, Inc.

Joseph S. Phillips and Susan J. Wood, Ph.D, Publishers
www.blackwidowpress.com

Cover Art: *Phase Portrait (6)* by Terry Winters
Cover Design: Kerrie Kemperman
Typesetting: Kerrie Kemperman

ISBN-13: 978-0-9842640-8-7

Printed in the United States

10 9 8 7 6 5 4 3 2 1

Our gratitude to the following magazines and literary blogs which published some of these translations: *Jacket* (Australia), *New American Writing, Bookslut, Ezra, Poetry & Poetics, The Brooklyn Rail, Guernica, Esque,* and *Cerise* (Paris).

Our thanks as well to Eric Lorberer and Kelly Everding at *Rain Taxi* for bringing out the serial poem "Daydream" in an OHM Editions chapbook in December 2010.

TABLE OF CONTENTS

A DOUBLE INTRODUCTION

I first heard of Bei Dao from Eliot Weinberger when in 1992 he called me and asked to nominate him for the semester-long MacAndless Chair in the Humanities, at Eastern Michigan University, where I taught from 1986 until my retirement in 2003. Eliot said that Bei Dao had been living in Scandinavia since his exile from China in 1989—when democracy and workers' rights activists shouted lines from his poems at the Tiananmen Square demonstrations—and was unhappy there, so Eliot wanted to help him try the USA. I nominated him for the Chair and he was offered the position to come in the fall of 1993. After his arrival, my wife Caryl and I found him a room in the home of our handyman, Barry LaRue, and Caryl worked with Marcia Dalbey, the Head of the English Department at EMU, to sort his immigration papers and apply for a Green Card. In 1994, Bei Dao, no longer affiliated with EMU, moved from Ypsilanti to Ann Arbor to share an apartment with a Chinese friend, staying on for two years before moving to Davis, California, where he had accepted a one-year position in East Asian Languages & Cultures at UC-Davis. Caryl and I saw a great deal of Bei Dao while he was in Ypsilanti/Ann Arbor. Bei Dao and I gave a number of poetry readings together and at two points I helped him translate some César Vallejo and Aimé Césaire poems, as well as some of my own, into Chinese. As a member of the English Department's Visiting Authors Committee, I invited Eliot Weinberger and Bei Dao translator David Hinton to campus for a reading of Bei Dao's poetry.

My introduction to Bei Dao's poetry was *The August Sleep-walker*, a "selected poetry," in effect, from 1972 to 1986, published by New Directions in 1992, and translated by Bonnie S. McDougall. I immediately sensed a floating rapport between some of the poems in *The August Sleepwalker* and César Vallejo's collection *Trilce*, which I had published a translation of in 1992. For example, here is section XII, in our translation, from Bei Dao's poem, "Daydream" (a serial poem with twenty-three sections which ends *The August Sleepwalker*, the longest poem he has ever published):

> A white gown drifts toward a
> place that does not exist
> the heart like a pump jerking in the summer night
> venting without cause
> the dusk banquet has ended
> the mountain ranges scatter
> mayflies write poems on water
> the horizon's odes stop and start
> a shadow is never the history of a man
> masks are fitted on or taken off
> flowers are born contingent
> lies are inseparable from grief
> if there were no masks
> why would clocks exist?
>
> when souls on the cliff reveal their primal forms
> only birds will recognize them

When I break this set of lines down into separate thoughts, here is one possible arrangement:

A white gown drifts toward a
place that does not exist

the heart like a pump jerking in the summer night
venting without cause

the dusk banquet has ended
mountain ranges scatter
mayflies write poems on water
the horizon's odes stop and start

a shadow is never the history of a man

masks are fitted on or taken off

flowers are born contingent

lies are inseparable from grief

if there were no masks
why would clocks exist

when souls on the cliff reveal their primal forms
only birds will recognize them

Possibly nine thoughts, or focuses, in sixteen lines. How-
ever, the sequitur non-sequitur lines are blurred. It would be
possible to assert that the following 4 lines are not non-sequitur
but a cluster of associated sensations/perceptions:

a shadow is never the history of a man
masks are fitted on or taken off
flowers are born contingent
lies are inseparable from grief

If a shadow is never a man's history, suggesting that it is a false version of the man, then it is a kind of mask. On the other hand, flowers are part of a natural process that is without duplicity. Unlike masks and faces, lies and grief are inseparable. And in the following couplet, the masks reappear and are set against a pointed and thoughtful question: were there to be no disguises, how could time exist? Implication: were all to be as it seems to be, might not time disappear? Might not clock time be contingent upon the concealment or the evocation of the gods? I am unsure where such questions lead, if anywhere. But they are provocative and thoughtful.

It is also possible to propose that the above Bei Dao passage can be read as the description of a situation followed by a commentary. The first eight lines evoke a state of mind, a dislocated speaker, heart-broken, alone in the mountains after a banquet, sensing poetry in the mayflies and the horizon. The second eight lines are his attempt to wrest meaning from his situation, to find in negation form and significance. Such a poem brings to mind the great art of Chinese landscape painting: among lofty and craggy peaks, tiny human figures. Here one could translate the cultural bureaucrats' dismissive term for Bei Dao and many of his contemporaries, *menglong*, or "misty" into a conjuring up of poets among fog-shrouded peaks.

Here in my translation is Vallejo's poem #XVI from *Trilce*. It is untitled.

> I have faith in being strong.
> Give me, armless air, give me leave
> to galloon myself with zeros on the left.
> And you, dream, give me your implacable diamond,
> your untimely time.
>
> I have faith in being strong.
> Over there advances a concave woman,
> a colorless quantity, whose grace
> closes where I open.

Into the air, friar past! Crabs, dolt!
The green presidential flag is glimpsed,
lowering the six remaining flags,
all the hangings of the return.

I have faith that I am,
And that I've been less.

Hey! A good start!

The Vallejo is at once more clear and more obscure than
the lines I have quoted from Bei Dao. The faith-in-oneself state-
ment, repeated three times, is set against examples of self-deco-
ration, the power of dreams, ambiguous feminine presence, the
antiquated religious past, and societal pomp. There is an Im-
pressionist quality to Bei Dao's lines that I do not sense in those
of Vallejo, whose writing in *Trilce* is more assertive, declarative
and jagged than most of the writing in *The August Sleepwalker*.
However, these two collections have a lot in common: both
poets are deeply involved in atmosphere, mood, and transitory
feelings, moving through their poems via associative nuances
that at times overlap and fuse, and that at other times appear to
be in exile from other aspects of the poem.[1]

Bei Dao and I were both invited to Naropa for a week in the
summer of 2009, and, as in the past, I was asked to do a program
with him, reading translations from his various New Directions
collections. While rereading translations of his poetry from the
1990s, not only by Bonnie S. McDougall and David Hinton,
but by Hinton and Yangbin Chen, Yangbin Chen by himself
and with John Rosenwald, I began to feel that new translations
might be able to draw out aspects of Bei Dao's poetry that were
not fully articulated by these earlier versions. I felt that Bei Dao
might be more complex and dense than he had been previously
rendered, and that it might be possible to do new versions that
were more substantial and yet still accurate. I believe that a poem

should be translated as often as possible, and not only by the same translator (as I had been doing with Vallejo for decades) but by other translators. During their lifetimes, poets such as Rainer Maria Rilke, Pablo Neruda, and Paul Celan were each translated by a number of translators. In the case of Rilke and Celan, who wrote in German (a language which I do not read), over the years I have laid out different translations side by side, and with a bilingual dictionary, attempted to get some sense of what they were about. By reading various translators' handling of a single poem and checking their word choices with dictionaries, I think it is possible to learn much more about a particular poem than by reading one translator's version of it.

Because I have been impressed by Lucas Klein's translation-oriented online *CipherJournal*, and knew that he admired Bei Dao's poetry, I suggested that we try working together. Lucas thought such might work so we decided to see what we could do. Since I do not read Chinese, we determined that he would do a first draft of a poem, pointing out ambiguities and complications, and that based on this information I would do a second draft, asking Lucas about the aspects of his draft that I did not understand. And so we would work, back and forth, until we arrived at a version that satisfied both of us. After doing a half dozen translations for the Naropa reading, with Bei Dao's approval and encouragement, we decided to continue and do a small collection, mainly from *Forms of Distance* and *Landscape Over Zero*. To the twenty-eight poems from these two collections, we have added several earlier pieces, including Bei Dao's famous "The Reply," and a version of "Daydream," to our reading an important bridge piece between the earlier poetry of the 1980s and that of the 1990s.   —Clayton Eshleman

***

In November, 1990, a review of Bei Dao's first book in *The New Republic* faulted the Chinese poet for writing that was too translatable.[2] This echoed some of the critiques leveled at Bei

Dao by the Chinese literary establishment of the early '80s, when his work first began to reach a wide readership, that he was writing "for translation." But at a conference in Denmark in October 1991, Bei Dao turned their criticisms on their ear: rather than writing for translation, or to be translated, Bei Dao was writing in what he called a "translation style,"[3] which is to say that he was writing against the predominant modes of Chinese literature by internalizing the use of language he had encountered in translations of North American, European, and Latin American writers (to call the prescribed politicization of language as found in Socialist-Realism under Chairman Mao a "predominant mode" is an understatement; nevertheless, in its domination it contained the seeds of its undoing: Bei Dao read the translations that would inspire and instruct his own style in clandestine books of foreign literature for "internal [i.e. within the Party] circulation," so cadres and bureaucrats could stay abreast of intellectual currents in the rest of the world).

Of course, the facts of world history have forced certain facts of literary history: while Bei Dao's poems are again publishable in China, and he now teaches creative writing at the Chinese University of Hong Kong, for the past two decades the majority of his readership has been in translation. These translations—as all translations do—reveal certain styles and stylistic choices of his translators, to which we present a small collection of alternatives. Fortunately, the language of Bei Dao—which Dutch scholar Maghiel van Crevel calls "lapidary,"[4] or chiseled and polished—is intricate and demanding enough that its origins in translation also withstand—or demand—further translations and re-translations into languages such as English. And since his books of the early- and mid-nineties represent his most focused efforts to wrestle with the issues of translation, translatability, and his new-found linguistic exile, we have decided to present our own translations of some of his poems from that era that show these questions most explicitly at work.

Bei Dao's poetry demands translation and re-translation not because it is so translatable, or written for a foreign audience, but rather because—in developing from literature in translation—it is so resistant to translation. In avoiding punctuation and playing with enjambment, lineation, and phrase-pacing, Bei Dao's poetry often sees a tension between a line and its surroundings—is its grammar self-contained, or subordinate to that of the stanza, or an extension of the line that precedes it, or follows it?—and very often each reading proposes its own alternate version. In our translations, our method has been, to as great an extent as possible, to re-cast that ambiguity and tension, rather than to resolve it in our English.

To get as close as possible to the ambiguities and tensions in Bei Dao's poetry is the main reason I agreed to go into these translations with Clayton. While most of my research in Chinese poetry has focused on the medieval period, I've also balanced this against studies of modern and contemporary Chinese poetry. This has meant that I've come into contact with a good deal of writing written under, or at times against, Bei Dao's influence—which, despite the difficulty of finding his writing in China for the past twenty years, has stayed strong—though I have to confess that I often found such influence opaque, even obscure. Working through these translations, however, has afforded me a chance to look at Bei Dao's poetry at a deeper level than I'd previously allowed myself. Too often I was reading the available translations just to check for mistakes, rather than to understand them as interpretations of Bei Dao's poetry. I now feel that I not only understand the translations by McDougall, Hinton, and others better, I am also able to present my own understanding, which has emerged through cooperation with Clayton and Bei Dao.

In our appendix, we present our back-and-forth over how to translate Bei Dao's poem "Untitled," the first line of which we have translated, after many visions and revisions, as "A hundred thousand windows shimmer." The poem, like so many, seems like a touchstone for Bei Dao's poetics, and not only for how the word for "shimmer" in Chinese is also associated with "ambiguous language." Windows, which we imagine to be transparent, end up taking on a texture of their own, reflecting and refracting when we want them to be clear. Language, too, is like this, especially in Bei Dao's poetic chiseling and polishing. We hope that our versions (translation, too, is an act that has often been compared against windows) also present not only a transparent vision of Bei Dao's "translation style" but a shimmering portal with its own reflective texture, as well.

—Lucas Klein

[1] *Trilce* was published in Lima, Peru, in 1922, with poetic procedures so radical for its time and place that it was for nearly all Peruvian readers unreadable. Bei Dao, and his generation of poets, working off Chinese translations of early 20th-century European and Latin American poets, as an alternative to folkloric and socialist realist poetry, found themselves, in their own way, in a kind of *Trilce*-like situation. However, because their writing in English translation was quite readable for contemporary European and American poets, a number of them have been read, reviewed, and discussed. We can appreciate their work for one reason because the "language poetry" of *Trilce* has had fifty years to percolate through Western consciousness.

[2] Stephen Owen, "The Anxiety of Global Influence—What is World Poetry?" in *The New Republic*, 203: 21 (Nov. 19, 1990), 28-32.

[3] Cf. Bei Dao, "Translation Style: A Quiet Revolution," Wei Deng, trans., in Wendy Larson and Anne Wedell-Wedellsborg, *Inside Out: Modernism and Postmodernism in Chinese Literary Culture* (Aarhus: Aarhus University Press, 1993), 60-64.

[4] Cf. Steve Bradbury, "'More than Writing, As We Speak': an Interview with Maghiel van Crevel on the Chinese Poetic Avant-Garde," in *Full Tilt: A Journal of East-Asian Poetry, Translation and the Arts* 4, <fulltilt.ncu.edu.tw>.

八月的夢游者

The August Sleepwalker

回答

卑鄙是卑鄙者的通行證，
高尚是高尚者的墓誌銘，
看吧，在那鍍金的天空中，
飄滿了死者彎曲的倒影。

冰川紀過去了，
為什麼到處都是冰凌？
好望角發現了，
為什麼死海裏千帆相競？

我來到這個世界上，
只帶着紙、繩索和身影，
為了在審判之前，
宣讀那被判決了的聲音：

告訴你吧，世界
我—不—相—信！
縱使你腳下有一千名挑戰者，
那就把我算作第一千零一名。

我不相信天是藍的，
我不相信雷的回聲，
我不相信夢是假的，
我不相信死無報應。

如果海洋注定要決堤，
就讓所有的苦水都注入我心中，
如果陸地注定要上升，
就讓人類重新選擇生存的峰頂。

新的轉機和閃閃星斗，
正在綴滿沒有遮攔的天空，
那是五千年的象形文字，
那是未來人們凝視的眼睛。

20

THE REPLY

Contempt is the passport of the contemptible,
gravitas is the epitaph of the grave,
see, in this aureate sky,
the drifting, bent reflections of the dead.

They say that the glacial era has passed,
why then is ice everywhere?
The Cape of Good Hope has been sighted,
why do a thousand ships still clash on the Dead Sea?

I have come into this world
bringing only paper, cord, and shadow,
to defend before the trial
those voices that have been judged:

I tell you, world,
I—do—not—believe!
Be there a thousand challengers underfoot,
count me as number one thousand and one.

I do not believe the sky is blue,
I do not believe the thunder's echoes,
I do not believe that dreams falsify,
I do not believe in death without retribution.

If the sea is doomed to smash the embankments
let all the brack dump into my heart;
if dry land is doomed to rise
let all humanity claim a new summit.

A new turn for the better with twinkling stars
is being stitched into the unbarricaded sky—
it is an ideogram five thousand years old,
staring eyes, the people of tomorrow.

白日夢

1
在秋天的暴行之後
這十一月被冰霜麻醉
展平在牆上
影子重重疊疊
那是骨骼石化的過程
你沒有如期歸來
我喉嚨裏的果核
變成了溫暖的石頭

我，行迹可疑
新的季節的閱兵式
敲打我的窗戶
住在鐘裏的人們
帶着擺動的心髒奔走
我俯視時間
不必轉身
一年的黑暗在杯中

2
音樂釋放的藍色靈魂
在煙蒂上飄搖
出入門窗的裂縫

一個準備切開的蘋果
—那裏沒有核兒
沒有生長敵意的種子
遠離太陽的磁場
玻璃房子裏生長的頭髮
如海藻，避開真實的

風暴，我們是
迷失在航空港裏的兒童
總想大哭一場

DAYDREAM

1

After autumn's savageries
November is anaesthetized by frost
flattened against the wall
shadows overlap and overlay
in a process of skeletal petrification
you did not come back as you said you would
the fruit pit in my throat
has become a warm stone

me, in surreptitious motion
the new season's military parade
knocking at my window
people who dwell in clocks
move with pendulous hearts
I look down on time
with no need to turn
the year's darkness inside a cup

2

Blue spirit released by music
wavers over a cigarette butt
in and out of the crack of the door

an apple ready for slicing
—there is no core there
no seed for growing hostility
far from the sun's magnetic field
hair grows in the glass house
like seaweed, evading a real

storm, so we are
children lost in a terminal
wanting to cry

在寬銀幕般的騷亂中
收集煙塵的鼻子
踫到了一起
說個不停：這是我
是我
我，我們

3
喃喃夢囈的
書，排列在一起
在早晨三點鐘
等待異端的火焰

時間並不憂鬱
我們棄絕了山林湖泊
集中在一起
為什麼我們在一起
一隻鐵皮烏鴉
在大理石的底座下
那永恆的事物的焊接處
不會斷裂

人們從石棺裏醒來
和我坐在一起
我們生前與時代合影
掛在長桌盡頭

4
你沒有如期歸來
而這正是離別的意義
一次愛的旅行
有時候就像抽煙那樣
簡單

in wide-screen riots
noses inhaling dust and smoke
collide
and cannot stop claiming: this is me
is me,
me, us

3
A book of
muttering sleeptalk compiled
at 3 A.M.
awaiting the flames of dissidence

time is not depressed
we have abandoned the mountains, forests, and lakes
bringing them together
why are we together
a tin crow
on a marble pedestal
the eternal seal of things
will never crack

people wake up in stone coffins
and sit by us
our pre-death group photo with the epoch
hangs at the end of the long table

4
You did not come back as you said you would
this is the true meaning of parting
a voyage of momentary love
is sometimes as simple
as smoking

地下室空守着你
內心的白銀
水仙花在暗中燦然開放
你聽憑所有的壞天氣
發怒、哭喊
乞求你打開窗戶

書頁翻開
所有的文字四散
只留下一個數字
—我的座位號碼
靠近窗戶
本次列車的終點是你

5
向日葵的帽子不翼而飛
石頭圓滑、可靠
保持着本質的完整
在沒有人居住的地方
山也變得年輕
晚鐘不必解釋什麼
巨蟒在蛻皮中進化
—繩索打結
把魚群懸掛在高處
一潭死水召來無數閃電
虎豹的斑紋漸呈藍色
天空已被吞噬

歷史靜默
峭壁目送着河上
那自源頭漂流而下的孩子
這人類的孩子

in the cellar vainly watching over
your innermost heart's silver
a narcissus blooms brightly in the dark
you permit all the bad weather
it rages and howls
begging you to open a window

the book's pages turn
scattering all the words
leaving behind only a number
—my seat number
next to the window
the terminus for this train is you

5

The sunflower's hat vanishes without a trace
the stone is evasively smooth and dependable
preserving a complete quality
in a place where no one lives
even the mountains are growing younger
the late bell explains nothing
the boa constrictor evolves while molting
—the ropes knot up
and hang fish in high places
a pool of dead water summons unending lightning
gradually the leopard's spots turn blue
the sky is already devoured

history is silent
the precipice observes the child adrift
down the river from the source
of humanity this is the child

6
我需要廣場
一片空曠的廣場
放置一個碗，一把小匙
一隻風箏孤單的影子

佔據廣場的人說
這不可能

籠中的鳥需要散步
夢游者需要貧血的陽光
道路撞擊在一起
需要平等的對話

人的衝動壓縮成
鈾，存放在可靠的地方

在一家小店鋪
一張紙幣，一片剃刀
一包劇毒的殺蟲劑
誕生了

7
我死的那年十歲
那拋向空中的球再也沒
落到地上
你是唯一的目擊者
十歲，我知道
然後我登上
那輛運載野牛的火車
被列入過期的提貨單里
供人們閱讀

今天早上
一隻鳥穿透我打開的報紙
你的臉嵌在其中

6

I need a public square
a wide-open square
to place a bowl on, a little spoon,
and a kite's lonesome shadow

the people occupying the square say
it cannot be done

a caged bird needs to walk
sleepwalkers need anemic sunlight
colliding roads
seek a reciprocal dialogue

people's impulses compressed into
uranium, store it somewhere safe

in some shop
a bill, a razor
and a pack of extra-strength bug killer
are born

7

The year I died I was ten
the ball hurled up into the sky never
fell
you were the sole witness
ten years old, I knew
afterwards I climbed onto the train
transporting wild oxen
and was listed in past-due invoices
for others to read

this morning
a bird flew through my open newspaper
where your face was inlaid

一種持久的熱情
仍在你的眼睛深處閃爍
我將永遠處於
你所設計的陰影中

8
多少年
多少火中的逃亡者
使日月無光
白馬展開了長長的繃帶
木樁釘進了煤層
滲出殷紅的血
毒蜘蛛彈撥它的琴弦
從天而降
開闊地，火球滾來滾去

多少年
多少條河流乾涸
露出那隱秘的部分
這是座空蕩蕩的博物館
誰置身其中
誰就會自以為是展品
被無形的目光注視
如同一顆琥珀爆炸後
飛出的沉睡千年的小蟲

9
終於有一天
謊言般無畏的人們
從巨型收音機裏走出來
讚美着災難
醫生舉起白色的床單
站在病樹上疾呼：
是自由，沒有免疫的自由
毒害了你們

long-lasting passion
deep in your eyes still flickers
I will remain forever
in the shadows you design

8
For how many years
how many fugitives from fire
have darkened both the sun and the moon
the white horse unwrapped a long bandage
the wooden stake piercing the coal bed
was seeping crimson blood
venomous spiders pluck their harp strings
as they descend from the sky
onto open ground, fire balls rolling all around

for how many years
how many rivers have run dry
exposing their private parts
this is an empty museum
anyone placed inside
will think himself on exhibit
eyed by imperceptible eyes
like an insect bolting from a thousand-year sleep
upon the amber's explosion

9
Finally one day
people fearless as lies
walked out of the giant radio
hailing catastrophe
the doctor lifted up a white bedsheet
stood on a sick tree and intoned:
it's freedom, from which no one is immune
that poisons you

存在的僅僅是聲音
一些簡單而細弱的聲音
就像單性繁殖的生物一樣
它們是古鐘上銘文的
合法繼承者
英雄、丑角、政治家
和腳踝纖細的女人
紛紛隱身於這聲音之中

10
手在喘息
流蘇在呻吟
雕花的窗櫺互相交錯
紙燈籠穿過遊廊
在盡頭熄滅
一支箭敲響了大門

牌位接連倒下
─連鎖反應的惡夢
子孫們
是威嚴的石獅嘴裏
腐爛的牙齒

當年鎖住風光的庭院
只剩下一棵樹
他們在酒後失態
圍着樹跳舞
瘋狂是一種例外

11
別把你的情欲帶入秋天
這殘廢者的秋天
打着響亮呼哨的秋天

what exists is mere sound
simple, frail sounds
like asexually reproducing organisms
the legal descendants
of the inscriptions on ancient bells
heroes, buffoons, politicians
and delicate-ankled women
disappear in turn in this sound

10
Hands wheeze
macramé whines
the lattice engravings interlock
paper lanterns pass along the promenade
to be snuffed at the end
an arrow thuds into the gate

memorial tablets fall like dominoes
—a chain reaction nightmare
the descendants
are the teeth rotting
in the maws of imposing stone lions

in the court that locked down what that year saw
a single tree remains
in drunken abandon
they reel about that tree
to go mad is a kind of exception

11
Don't bring your lust into autumn
this autumn of cripples
autumn of reverberating whistles

一隻女人乾燥的手
掠過海面，卻滴水未沾
推移礁石的晚霞
是你的情欲
焚燒我

我，心如枯井
對海洋的渴望使我遠離海洋
走向我的開端—你
或你的盡頭—我

我們終將迷失在大霧中
互相呼喚
在不同的地點
成為無用的路標

12
白色的長袍飄向那
不存在的地方
心如夏夜裏抽搐的水泵
無端地發泄
黃昏的晚宴結束了
山巒散去
蜉蝣在水上寫詩
地平線的頌歌時斷時續
影子並非一個人的歷史
戴上或摘下面具
花朵應運而生
謊言與悲哀不可分離
如果沒有面具
所有鐘表還有什麼意義

當靈魂在岩石是顯出原形
只有鳥會認出它們

the dry hand of a woman
skims the sea's surface but doesn't get wet
forcing back reefs the rosy dusk clouds
are your lust
lighting me on fire

me, heart like a dry well
kept from the sea by my thirst for the sea
walking toward my beginning—you
or toward your ending—me

we'll end up lost in the fog
shouting to each other
from different spots
becoming useless road signs

12
A white gown drifts toward a
place that does not exist
the heart like a pump jerking in the summer night
venting without cause
the dusk banquet has ended
mountain ranges scatter
mayflies write poems on water
the horizon's odes stop and start
a shadow is never the history of a man
masks are fitted on or taken off
flowers are born contingent
lies are inseparable from grief
if there were no masks
why would clocks exist?

when souls on the cliff reveal their primal forms
only birds will recognize them

13
他指着銀色的沼澤說
那裏發生過戰爭
幾棵冒煙的樹在地平線飛奔
轉入地下的士兵和馬
閃着磷光，日夜
追隨着將軍的鎧甲

而我們追隨的是
思想的流彈中
那逃竄着的自由的獸皮

昔日陣亡者的頭顱
如殘月升起
越過沙沙作響的灌木叢
以預言家的口吻說
你們並非倖存者
你們永無歸宿

新的思想呼嘯而過
擊中時代的背影
一滴蒼蠅的血讓我震驚

14
我注定要坐在岸邊
在一張白紙上
期待着老年斑似的詞

出現，秩序與混亂
蜂房釀造着不同的情欲
九十九座紅色的山峰

上漲，空氣稀薄
地衣居心叵測地蔓延
渺小，猶如塵世的

36

13

He points to a silvery swamp and says
there was a war there
trees spewing smoke rush over the horizon
the soldiers and horses slipped underground
shine phosphorescent, day and night
trailing the general's armor

but what we trail is
the scampering and free animal hide
amidst the stray bullets of ideology

the skulls of yesteryear's killed-in-action
rise a waning moon
they leap past the rustling shrubs
to intone like a prophet
you are not the survivors
you will never reach home

a new ideology comes whistling by
smacking the era's back
a drop of fly's blood has left me jolted

14

I am doomed to sit by the shore
on a blank sheet of paper
anticipated words like spots of senile plaque

appear, order and chaos
this beehive brews multiple lusts
ninety-nine red mountaintops

rise, the air thins
unpredictable lichen spreads its ill-intent
negligible, an artifice exists

計謀，鋼筋支撐着權力
石頭也會暈眩
這畢竟是一種可怕的

高度，白紙背面
孩子的手在玩影子遊戲
光源來自海底兩條交尾的
電鰻

15
蹲伏在瓦罐裏的夜
溢出清涼的
水，那是我們愛的源泉

回憶如傷疤
我的一生在你的腳下
這流動的沙丘
凝聚在你的手上
成為一顆眩目的鑽石

沒有床，房間
小得使我們無法分離
四壁薄如棉紙
數不清的嘴巴畫在牆上
低聲輪唱

你沒有如期歸來
我們共同啜飲的杯子
砰然碎裂

16
礦山廢棄已久
它的金屬拉成細長的線

貓頭鷹透體通明
胃和神經叢掠過夜空

like this world of dust, power propped up by rebar
even the stones get dizzy
this is after all a frightening

altitude, under the blank sheet's backside
a child's hand forms shadows
coupling beneath the sea electric eels
create the light

15
Night squatting in a terra-cotta jug
overflowed cool clear
water, the source of our love

memory like a scar
my entire life is under your feet
this drifting dune
congeals in your hand
becomes a dazzling diamond

with no bed, the room is
so small we cannot draw apart
tissue paper thin walls
with countless mouths drawn on them
singing barely audible rounds

you did not come back as you said you would
the cup from which we had sipped
snaps into slivers

16
The mine has long been abandoned
its metals attenuated into long wires

light shines through the owl
its stomach and nerve fibers skim the night sky

古生物的聯盟解體了
粘合化石的工作

仍在進行，生存
永遠是一種集體冒險

生存永遠是和春天
在進行戰爭

綠色的履帶碾過
陰鬱的文明

噴射那水銀的噴泉
金屬的頭改變了地貌

安詳無夢

17
幾個世紀過去了
一日尚未開始
冷空氣觸摸了我的手
螺旋樓梯般上升
黑與白，光線
在房瓦的音階上轉換
一棵棗樹的安寧
男人的喉嚨成熟了

動物園的困獸
被合進一本本書裏
鋼鞭飛舞
悸動着的斑斕色彩
隔着漫長的歲月
淒厲地叫喊
一張導游圖把我引入

the paleontological union breaks up
the work of fusing fossils

continues, existence
has always been a collective adventure

existence has always been at war
with spring

green tractor-treads have flattened
a depressed civilization

the metal head of that mercury-spewing
spout has changed the dreamless

topographical serenity

17
Centuries have passed
but a single day has yet to begin
cold air brushes my hand
and ascends like a spiral stair
black and white, rays of light
transform on the musical scale of the roof tiles
into the tranquility of a jujube tree
the throats of men have matured

the pent beasts in the zoo
have been walled up in book after book
steel whips flicker
a kaleidoscopic throb
obstructed by unending years
forlorn wails
a tourist map guides me into

城中之城
星星狡黠而兇狠
像某一事件的核心

18
我總是沿着那條街的
孤獨的意志漫步
喔，我的城市
在玻璃的堅冰上滑行

我的城市我的故事
我的水龍頭我的積怨
我的鸚鵡我的
保持平衡的睡眠

罌粟花般芳香的少女
從超級市場飄過
帶着折刀般表情的人們
共飲冬日的寒光

詩，就像陽台一樣
無情地折磨着我
被煙塵粉刷的牆
總在意料之中

19
當你轉身的時候
花崗岩崩裂成細細的流沙
你用陌生的語調
對空曠說話，不真實
如同你的笑容

深深植入昨天的苦根
是最黑暗處的閃電

the city within the city
the stars are vicious and sly
like a certain incident at its core

18
I'm forever strolling along that street's
lonely volition
oh, my city
slides on glass's hard ice

my city my stories
my faucet my rancor
my parrot my
equilibrious sleep

a girl as fragrant as poppies
floats out of the supermarket
urging people with pocketknife expressions
to imbibe winter's clashing light

poetry like a balcony
mercilessly tormenting me
walls painted by smoke and dust
inevitably impending

19
When you turn around
granite splinters into quicksand
in a stranger's tone you
address the void, as unreal as
your smile

the bitter roots deeply planted into yesterday
are the darkest places' lightning

擊中了我們想像的巢穴
從流沙的瀑布中
我們聽見了水晶撞擊的音樂

一次小小的外科手術
我們挖掘矬石的雪地上
留下了麻雀的爪印
一輛冬天瘋狂的馬車
穿過夏日的火焰

我們安然無恙
四季的美景
印在你的衣服上

20
放牧是一種觀點的陳述
熱病使羊群膨脹
像一個個氣球上升
卡在天蠍星座中
熱風卷走了我的屋頂
在四壁之內
我靜觀無字的天空
文化是一種共生現象
包括羊的價值
狼的原則
鐘罩裏一無所有
在我們的視野里
只有一條乾涸的河道
幾縷筆直的煙
古代聖賢們
無限寂寞
垂釣着他們的魚

assaulting the lair of our imaginations
in the cataract of quicksand
we hear the sound of crystals crashing

a minor surgery
sparrow tracks are left in the snow
over our flint excavations
a winter-crazed horse cart
jolts through the flames of summer

we are safe and sound
the scenery of all four seasons
printed on your clothing

20
Shepherding is the declaration of a viewpoint
heatstroke swells the sheep up
like balloons ascending one after another
stuck in Scorpio
a hot gust ripped away my roof
inside these four walls
I meditate on the wordless sky
culture is a symbiotic phenomenon
that includes the value of sheep
and the principles of wolves
there is nothing under the bell jar
in our field of vision
there's merely a dry riverbed
a few wisps of straightening smoke
in limitless solitude
ancient sages
angled for some fish

21
詭秘的豆莢有五隻眼睛
它們不願看見白晝
只在黑暗裏傾聽

一種顏色是一個孩子
誕生時的啼哭

宴會上桌布潔白
杯中有死亡的味道
—悼詞揮發的沉悶氣息

傳統是一張航空照片
山河縮小成樺木的紋理

總是人，俯首聽命於
說教、效倣、爭鬥
和他們的尊嚴

尋找激情的旅行者
穿過候鳥荒涼的棲息地

石膏像打開窗戶
藝術家從背後
用工具狠狠地敲碎它們

22
弱音器弄啞了的小號
忽然響亮地哭喊
那偉大悲劇的導演
正悄悄死去
兩隻裝着滑輪的獅子
仍在固定的軌道上
東奔西撞

21
Sneaky peapods have five eyes
they're unwilling to look into the sunlight
rather they eavesdrop in the dark

a color is a child's
cry at birth

the banquet tablecloth a pristine white
the flavor of death in the cups
—testimonials vaporize the repugnant odors

tradition is a photo of a bird's eye view
mountains and rivers shrunk to birch grain

it's always people, heads bowing and obeying
sermons, mimicry, struggle
and their own dignity

travelers on a quest for passion
pass by the desolate haunts of migrating birds

plaster statues open the windows
while from behind the artist
ruthlessly smashes them with his tools

22
A muted trumpet
suddenly blares
the director of that great tragedy
is quietly dying
two lions cranked in by pulleys
keep crashing left and right
on their unswerving tracks

曙光癱瘓在大街上
很多地址和名字和心事
在郵筒在夜裏避雨
貨車場的鴨子喧嘩
窗戶打着哈欠
一個來蘇水味的早晨
值班醫生填寫着死亡報告

悲劇的偉大意義啊
日常生活的瑣碎細節

23
在晝與夜之間出現了裂縫

語言突然變得陳舊
像第一場雪
那些用黑布蒙面的證人
緊緊包圍了你
你把一根根松枝插在地上
默默點燃它們

那是一種祭奠的儀式
從死亡的山岡上
我居高臨下
你是誰
要和我交換什麼
白鶴展開一張飄動的紙
上面寫着你的回答
而我一無所知

你沒有如期歸來

dawn light is paralyzed in the street
many addresses, names and worries
find shelter in a mailbox from night's rain
a clamor of ducks in the freight yard
the windows are yawning
on a morning stinking of Lysol
the doctor on duty fills out a death report

the great meaning of this tragedy, ay
the inane details of everyday life

23
A crack appears between morning and evening

language is suddenly obsolete
like first snow
witnesses masked with black cloth
encircle you tightly
you jam pine branches into the ground
and without speaking set them ablaze

this is a funereal rite
from the knoll of death
I peered down
who are you
what will you exchange with me
a white crane spreads out a fluttering sheet of paper
on which is written your reply
but I know nothing

you did not come back as you said you would

舊雪

Old Snow

布拉格

一群鄉下蛾子在攻打城市
街燈，幽靈的臉
細長的腿支撐着夜空

有了幽靈，有了歷史
地圖上未標明的地下礦脈
是布拉格粗大的神經

卡夫卡的童年穿過廣場
夢在逃學，夢
是坐在雲端的嚴厲的父親

有了父親，有了繼承權
一隻耗子在皇宮的走廊漫步
影子的侍從前簇後擁

從世紀大門出發的輕便馬車
途中變成了坦克
真理在選擇它的敵人

有了真理，有了遺忘
醉漢如雄蕊在風中搖晃
抖落了塵土的咒語

越過伏兒塔瓦河上時間的
橋，進入耀眼的白天
古老的雕像們充滿敵意

有了敵意，有了榮耀
小販神秘地攤開一塊絲絨
請買珍珠聚集的好天氣

PRAGUE

Swarming country moths assault the city
street lamps, spectral faces
long, slender legs holding up the night sky

there are specters, there is history
unmarked on the map a subterranean vein
is the thick nerve of Prague

Kafka's youth passed through the square
dreams are cutting class, dreams
are the stern father sitting in the clouds

there is a father, there are rights of inheritance
a rat is wandering the palace halls
attendants in the shadows a bustling entourage

a carriage setting out from the century's gate
turns into a tank midway
truth is selecting its enemies

there is truth, there is forgetting
a drunk quivering like a stamen in the breeze
shaking off the curse of dust

traversing the bridge of time over the Vltava
River, entering the daylit glare
the ancient statues are full of enmity

there is enmity, there is splendor
a vendor mysteriously unfolds a swatch of velvet
please purchase this fine weather gathered by pearls

在天涯

At the Sky's Edge

以外

瓶中的風暴率領着大海前進
碼頭以外，漂浮的不眠之床上
擁抱的情人接上權力的鏈條
畫框以外，帶古典笑容的石膏像
以一日之內的陰影說話
信仰以外，駿馬追上了死亡
月亮不停地在黑色事件上蓋章
故事以外，一棵塑料樹迎風招展
陰鬱的糧食是我們生存的借口

BEYOND

A bottled storm commands the sea advancing
beyond the dock,   on a bed afloat with insomnia
lovers embracing link up chains of power
beyond the painting's frame,   classically smiling plaster statues
use a single day's shadows to speak
beyond belief,   stallions have caught up with death
relentlessly the moon stamps its seal on black events
beyond the story,   a plastic tree trembles in the breeze
this dismal grain is the excuse for our existence

蘋果與頑石

大海的祈禱儀式
一個壞天氣俯下了身

頑石空守五月
抵抗着綠色傳染病

四季輪流砍伐着大樹
群星在辨認道路

醉漢以他的平衡術
從時間中突圍

一顆子彈穿過蘋果
生活已被借用

APPLE AND STUBBORN ROCK

The sea's prayer ritual
one bad weather bending down

in vain stubborn rock guards May
resisting the green contagion

the four seasons take turns axing trees
many stars are identifying the road

with his balancing skills the drunkard
breaks the inner siege of time

a bullet pierces an apple
life has been put on loan

毒藥

煙草屏住呼吸

流亡者的窗戶對準
大海深處放飛的翅膀
冬日的音樂駛來
像褪色的旗幟

是昨天的風，是愛情

悔恨如大雪般降落
當一塊石頭裸露出結局
我以此刻痛哭餘生

再給我一個名字

我偽裝成不幸
遮擋母語的太陽

POISON

Tobacco bates breath

the exile's window is aligned with
wings the sea's depths sent soaring
winter music sailing in
like a fading flag

is yesterday's wind, is love

regret descends like a heavy snowfall
in the moment a stone bares its finale
I wail out the rest of my life

give me one more name

I disguise myself as misfortune
I block out the sun of the mother tongue

在天涯

群山之間的愛情

永恒，正如萬物的耐心
簡化人的聲音
一聲淒厲的叫喊
從遠古至今

休息吧，疲憊的旅行者
受傷的耳朵
暴露了你的尊嚴

一聲淒厲的叫喊

AT THE SKY'S EDGE

Love between mountain ranges

eternity, like the patience of the 10,000 things,
simplifies the human sound
one strident cry
from the deep past to now

rest, weary voyager
lacerated ears
have exposed your dignity

one strident cry

播種者

一個播種者走進大廳
外面是戰爭，他說
而你沉湎於空虛
放棄警示危險的責任
我以田野的名義
外面是戰爭

我走出大廳
四周一片豐收的景象
我開始設計戰爭
表演死亡
被我點燃的莊稼
狼煙般升起

一個念頭讓我發瘋：
他正在大理石上播種

SOWER

A sower walks into the hall
it's war out there, he says
you are wallowing in vapidity
shirking your duty to warn of the danger
I am come in the name of the fields
it's war out there

I leave the hall
all around   scenes of the harvest
I start to design the war
to perform death
the crops I torch
flare up like wolf signals

one thought is driving me crazy:
he is sowing seeds onto marble

新世紀

傾心於榮耀，大地轉暗
我們讀混凝土之書的
燈光，讀真理

金子的炸彈爆炸
我們情願成為受害者
把傷口展示給別人

考古學家會發現
底片上的時代幽靈
一個孩子抓住它，說不

是歷史妨礙我們飛行
是鳥妨礙我們走路
是腿妨礙我們做夢

是我們誕生了我們
是誕生

A NEW CENTURY

Hearts leant to honor, the earth darkens
we read the light in the Book of
Cement, read the truth

the golden bomb explodes
we are willing to turn into victims
and to display our wounds to others

on some photo-negative an archeologist
will discover the spirit of the times
which a child grabs onto, saying no,

it is history that prevents us from flying
birds that prevent us from walking
legs that prevent us from dreaming

we who give birth to ourselves
who are birth

問天

今夜雨零亂
清風翻書
字典旁敲側擊
逼我就範

從小背古詩
不得要領
闡釋的深淵旁
我被罰站

月朗星稀
老師的手從中
指點迷津
影子戲仿人生

有人在教育
的斜坡上滑雪
他們的故事
滑出國界

詞滑出了書
白紙是遺忘症
我洗淨雙手
撕碎它，雨停

QUESTIONING HEAVEN

Tonight a messy rain
a cool breeze flips through a book
the dictionary is oblique with slander
and forces me to submit

as a child memorizing ancient poems
I never fully understood
and was sent to stand
by the abyss of explication

under a bright moon and scattered stars
the teacher's hand points
a way out of the labyrinth
while shadows mimic human life

on the slopes of education
there are people skiing
their stories
zoom beyond our borders

words zoom out of books
a white page is amnesia
I purge my hands
and tear it out, end of rain

忠誠

別開燈
黑暗之門引來聖者

我的手熟知途徑
像一把舊鑰匙
在心的位置
打開你的命運

三月在門外飄動

幾根竹子搖晃
有人正從地下潛泳
暴風雪己過
蝴蝶重新集結

我信仰般追隨你
你追隨死亡

LOYALTY

Don't turn on the light
the door of darkness is drawing in a saint

my hand is familiar with the path
as with an old key
at the heart's place
turning open your fate

March floats outside the door

bamboo stems are swaying
someone is swimming underground
the blizzard has passed
butterflies amass afresh

like a belief I follow you
you follow death

一幅肖像

為信念所傷，他來自八月
那危險的母愛
被一面鏡子奪去
他側身於犀牛與政治之間
像裂縫隔開時代

哦同謀者，我此刻
只是一個普通的遊客
在博物館大廳的棋盤上
和別人交叉走動

激情不會過時
但訪問必須秘密進行
我突然感到那琴絃的疼痛
你調音，為我奏一曲
在眾獸湧入歷史之前

A PORTRAIT

Hurt for belief, he comes from August
that dangerous maternal love
vanquished by a mirror
he sidles in between a rhinoceros and politics
the way a breach splits eras

oh accomplices, right now
I'm no more than a typical tourist
on the chessboard of a museum lobby
adrift intersecting with others

the passion will not turn passé
but visits must take place in secret
suddenly I feel the pangs of zither strings
you tune them up, strumming a song for me
before the rush of carnivores into history

關於永恒

從眾星租來的光芒下
長跑者穿過死城

和羊談心
我們共同分享美酒
和桌下的罪行

霧被引入夜歌
爐火如偉大的謠言
迎向風

如果死是愛的理由
我們愛不貞之情
愛失敗的人
那察看時間的眼睛

CONCERNING ETERNITY

Under light rented from the stars
distance runners cross the dead city

during a heart-to-heart with sheep
we share exquisite wine
and under-the-table guilt

fog has been drawn into our night songs
like a great rumor the stove fire
sends out greetings to the airs

if death is love's reason
then we love infidelity
love the defeated
whose eyes keep checking the time

零度以上的風景

The Landscape Above Zero Degrees

背景

必須修改背景
你才能夠重返故鄉

時間撼動了某些字
起飛，又落下
沒透露任何消息
一連串的失敗是捷徑
穿過大雪中寂靜的看臺
逼向老年的大鐘

而一個家庭宴會的高潮
和酒精的含量有關
離你最近的女人
總是帶着歷史的愁容
注視着積雪、空行

田鼠們所堅信的黑暗

BACKGROUND

Before you can return to your old home
you must correct the background

shaken by time certain words
take off, then land
without disclosing any information
a series of failures a shortcut
forcing its way through snowed-in bleachers
toward the great clock of old age

the climax of a family banquet
has to do with alcohol content
the woman closest to you
always wears history's anguished face
staring at snow banks and blank space

the darkness field mice insist on believing in

無題

在父親平坦的想像中
孩子們固執的叫喊
終於撞上了高山
不要驚慌
我沿着某些樹的想法
從口吃轉向歌唱

來自遠方的悲傷
是一種權力
我用它鋸桌子
有人為愛情出發
而一座宮殿追隨風暴
駛過很多王朝

帶傢俱的生活
此外，跳蚤擂動大鼓
道士們練習升天
青春深入小巷
為夜的邏輯而哭
我得到休息

UNTITLED

In a father's level imagination
the persistent cries of children
finally strike against a mountain
don't panic
I walk along the thoughts of certain trees
and turn from stuttering into song

sorrow that comes from afar
is a form of power
that I use to saw tables
some people depart for love
while a palace in pursuit of storms
journeys past many kingdoms

beyond life with
furniture, fleas beat a great drum
Daoist priests practice their ascent to heaven
youth pass down the lanes
sobbing over night's logic
I achieve rest

這一天

風熟知愛情
夏日閃爍着皇家的顏色
釣魚人孤獨地測量
大地的傷口
敲響的鐘在膨脹
午後的漫步者
請加入這歲月的含義

有人俯向鋼琴
有人扛着梯子走過
睡意被推遲了幾分鐘
僅僅幾分鐘
太陽在研究陰影
我從明鏡飲水
看見心目中的敵人

男高音的歌聲
像油輪激怒大海
我凌晨三時打開罐頭
讓那些魚大放光明

THIS DAY

The wind is intimate with love
summer shimmers with imperial colors
someone fishing lonesomely measures
the earth's wounds
the chiming clock is swelling
those of you strolling through the afternoon
please join in the meaning of the age

some people bow to a piano
others carry a ladder by
sleepiness has been checked for a few minutes
only a few minutes
the sun is researching the shadow
I quaff water from a bright mirror
and spot the enemy in my mind's eye

the tenor's singing
enrages the sea like an oil tanker
at 3 A.M. I open a can
releasing those fish into the light

二月

夜正趨於完美
我在語言中漂流
死亡的樂器
充滿了冰

誰在日子的裂縫上
歌唱，水變苦
火焰失血
山貓般奔向星星
必有一種形式
才能做夢

在早晨的寒冷中
一隻覺醒的鳥
更接近真理
而我和我的詩
一起下沉

書中的二月：
某些動作與陰影

FEBRUARY

The night is rushing to perfection
I drift inside language
the musical instruments of death
are filled with ice

who sings on the crevice
of days, water turns bitter
flames hemorrhage
pouncing like pumas to the stars
there must be form
for there to be dreams

in the chill of early morning
a wide-awake bird
gets closer to the truth
while my poems and I
sink as one

February in books:
certain movements certain shadows

我們

失魂落魄
提着燈籠追趕春天

傷疤發亮，杯子轉動
光線被創造
看那迷人的時刻：
盜賊潛入郵局
信發出叫喊

釘子啊釘子
這歌詞不可更改
木柴緊緊摟在一起
尋找聽眾

尋找冬天的心
河流盡頭
船夫等待着茫茫暮色

必有人重寫愛情

WE

scared out of our wits
carry lanterns chasing spring

scars gleam, cups rotate
rays of light are created
watch for that moment of bewitchery:
a thief steals into the post office
letters send out shrieks

nails oh nails
the words of this song will not be changed
firewood huddled closely
searching for an audience

searching for the heart of winter
the end of the stream
the boatman waits for all-penetrating dusk

someone has to rewrite love

明鏡

夜半飲酒時
真理的火焰發瘋
回首處
誰沒有家
窗戶為何高懸

你倦於死
道路倦於生
在那火紅的年代
有人晝伏夜行
與民族對弈

並不止於此
挖掘你睡眠的人
變成藍色
早晨倦於你
明鏡倦於詞語

想想愛情
你有如壯士
驚天動地之處
你對自己說
太冷

THE BRIGHT MIRROR

Drinking wine at midnight
the flame of truth goes crazy
looking back
who is homeless
why are the windows hung so high?

you are fed up with dying
the road is fed up with living
during that fire-red decade
someone hid by day and pushed on by night
and played Go with the nation

but there's more
the person digging out your sleep
has become blue
the morning is fed up with you
the bright mirror is fed up with terminology

thinking about love
you are like some heaven-
startling earthshaking hero
who says to himself
it's too cold

據我所知

前往那故事中的人們
搬開了一座大山
他才誕生

我從故事出發
剛抵達另一個國家
顛倒字母
使每餐必有意義

踮腳夠着時間的刻度
戰爭對他還太遠
父親又太近
他低頭通過考試
踏上那無邊的甲板

隔牆有耳
但我要攔上他的速度
寫作！

他用紅色油漆道路
讓鳳凰們降落
展示垂死的動作
那些含義不明的路標
環繞着冬天
連音樂都在下雪
我小心翼翼
每個字下都是深淵

AS FAR AS I KNOW

Only when those people advancing to the legend
cleared away its great mountain
was he born

I set out from that legend
to now arrive in another country
turning over alphabets
to pack each meal with meaning

on tiptoes to touch the mark of time
the war is still too distant
his father too close
he buries his head to pass a test
steps onto a boundless deck

the walls have ears
but I must match his speed
to write!

he paints the road red
allows the fenghuang making
signs of dying to descend
ambiguous roadsigns
encircle the winter
even music is snowing
I am extra careful
under each character is an abyss

當一棵大樹
平息着八面來風
他的花園
因妄想而荒蕪

我漫不經心地翻看
他的不良記錄
只能堅信過去的花朵

他偽造了我的簽名
而長大成人
並和我互換大衣
以潛入我的夜
搜尋着引爆故事的
導火索

when a huge tree
quells wind from all eight directions
his garden
goes to waste from fantasy

carelessly I flip through
his tarnished record
believing solely in flowers from the past

he forged my signature
to grow into a man
switched coats with me
to infiltrate my nights
searching for that legend's blasting
cap

守夜

月光小於睡眠
河水穿過我們的房間
傢俱在哪兒靠岸

不僅是編年史
也包括非法的氣候中
公認的一面
使我們接近雨林
哦哭泣的防線

玻璃鎮紙讀出
文字敘述中的傷口
多少黑山擋住了
一九四九年

在無名小調的盡頭
花握緊拳頭叫喊

NIGHTWATCH

Moonlight frailer than slumber
river water passes through our bedroom
where does the furniture pull ashore?

not only the chronicles
but the consensus of
a criminal atmosphere
move us closer to the rain forest
oh weeping line of defense

the glass paperweight detects
the wounds written out of the narrative
how many black mountains obstructed
1949?

at the end of an unnamed tune
fists clenched flowers scream

舊地

死亡總是從反面
觀察一幅畫

此刻我從窗口
看見我年輕時的落日
舊地重遊
我急於說出真相
可在天黑前
又能說出什麼

飲過詞語之杯
更讓人乾渴
與河水一起援引大地
我在空山傾聽
吹笛人內心的嗚咽

稅收的天使們
從畫的反面歸來
從那些鍍金的頭顱
一直清點到落日

THE OLD PLACE

Death always observes
a painting from behind

out this window right now
I see a sunset from my youth
an old place revisited
I'm eager to speak the truth
but before the sky darkens
what else can be said?

downing a cup of terminology
just makes one more parched
the river's water and I quote the earth
among empty mountains I listen in on
the whimpering of the flutist's inmost heart

the angels of taxation
return from behind the painting
ceaselessly sorting and counting until
sunset those aureate skulls

失眠

你在你的窗外看你
一生的光線變幻

因嫉妒而瞎了眼
星星逆風而行
在死亡的隱喻之外
展開道德的風景

在稱為源泉的地方
夜終於追上了你
那失眠的大軍
向孤獨的旗幟致敬

輾轉的守夜人
點亮那朵驚恐之花
貓縱身躍入長夜
夢的尾巴一閃

INSOMNIA

You are outside your window looking at your
whole life's fluctuating beams

eyes blinded out of jealousy
stars take off against the wind
surpassing death's metaphor
unfolding morality's landscape

at that place called Wellspring
the night finally catches up to you
its insomniac army
salutes the flag of solitude

passing over many lands the night watchman
illuminates the flowers of panic
a cat leaps into the long night
dream tail flashing once

零度以上的風景

是鷂鷹教會歌聲游泳
是歌聲追溯那最初的風

我們交換歡樂的碎片
從不同的方向進入家庭

是父親確認了黑暗
是黑暗通向經典的閃電

哭泣之門砰然關閉
回聲在追趕它的叫喊

是筆在絕望中開花
是花反抗着必然的旅程

是愛的光線醒來
照亮零度以上的風景

THE LANDSCAPE ABOVE ZERO DEGREES

It is the sparrow hawk who teaches song to swim
it is the song that retraces the earliest airs

we exchange fragments of delight
and enter the family from different routes

it is the father who has confirmed the dark
it is the dark that leads to the classics' lightning

the door of weeping shuts with a thud
leaving the echo to pursue its wail

it is the pen that flowers within despair
it is the flower that resists necessity's path

it is love's beam that awakes
to brighten the landscape above zero degrees

蠟

青春期的蠟
深藏在記憶的鎖內
火焰放棄了酒
廢墟上的匆匆過客
我們的心

我們的心
會比恨走得更遠
夜拒絕明天的讀者
被點燃的蠟燭
暈眩得像改變天空的
一陣陣鐘聲
此刻唯一的沉默

此刻唯一的沉默
是裸露的花園
我們徒勞地捲入其中
燭火比秋霧更深
漫步到天明

WAX

The wax of puberty
buried deep behind the lock of memory
the flame has surrendered its alcohol
the ruins are crossed by hurrying travelers
our hearts

our hearts
will surpass even hatred
the night rejects tomorrow's readers
the lit candle wax
dazzles like the sky-changing
toll upon toll of a bell
this moment's only silence

this moment's only silence
is an exposed garden
we have been pointlessly drawn into
denser than autumnal fog the candle flame
wanders until daybreak

關鍵詞

我的影子很危險
這受顧於太陽的藝人
帶來最後的知識
是空的

那是蛀蟲工作的
黑暗屬性
暴力的最小的孩子
空中的足音

關鍵詞，我的影子
捶打着夢中之鐵
踏着那節奏
一隻孤狼走進

無人失敗的黃昏
鷺鷥在水上書寫
一生一天一個句子
結束

KEYWORD

My shadow is dangerous
the performer employed by the sun
delivers final knowledge
which is empty

that is the dark nature
of the termite's work
the footsteps through the air
of the smallest child of violence

the keyword, my shadow,
hammers the iron inside dreams
stepping to the rhythms
a lone wolf walks in

the dusk undefeated by anyone
the egret that writes on the water
a life   a day   a sentence
ending

無題

千百個窗戶閃爍
這些預言者
在昨天與大海之間
哦迷途的歡樂

橋成為現實
跨越公共的光線
而涉及昨日玫瑰的
秘密旅行提供
一張紙一種困境

母親的淚我的黎明

UNTITLED

A hundred thousand windows shimmer
these soothsayers
are between yesterday and the sea
oh the joys of getting lost

a bridge becomes reality
spanning public rays of light
while the secret voyage touching
yesterday's rose provides
a dilemma for each sheet of paper

a dawn for each of my mother's tears

邊境

風暴轉向北方的未來
病人們的根在地下怒吼
太陽的螺旋槳
驅趕蜜蜂變成光芒
鏈條上的使者們
在那些招風耳裏播種

被記住的河流
不再終結
被偷去了的聲音
已成為邊境

邊境上沒有希望
一本書
吞下一個翅膀
還有語言的堅冰中
贖罪的兄弟
你為此而鬥爭

THE BORDER

The storm turns toward the future of the north
the roots of the sick wail underground
the sun's propeller
compels the bees to change into light
chains of envoys
scatter seeds into wind-snatching ears

streams remembered
will never end
sounds stolen
have become the border

at the border there is no hope
a book
gulps down a wing
and the atoning brothers
are inside the solid ice of language
for which you struggle

無題

醒來是自由
那星辰之間的矛盾

門在抵抗歲月
絲綢捲走了叫喊
我是被你否認的身份
從心裏關掉的燈

這脆弱的時刻
敵對的岸
風折疊所有的消息
記憶變成了主人

哦陳酒
因表達而變色
煤會遇見必然的礦燈
火不能為火作證

UNTITLED

To wake up is to be free
a contradiction among the stars

the door resists the years
screams are enrolled by silken scrolls
I am the identity you have denied
the light you have turned off in your heart

this brittle instant
these antagonistic shores
the wind enfolds all the news
memory becomes master

ah the old wine
expression has changed its color
coal meets the mine lamp of necessity
fire cannot testify for fire

冬之旅

誰在虛無上打字
太多的故事
是十二塊石頭
擊中錶盤
是十二隻天鵝
飛離冬天

而夜裏的石頭
描述着光線
盲目的鐘
為缺席者呼喊

進入房間
你看見那個丑角
在進入冬天時
留下的火焰

WINTER VOYAGE

Who is typing in the emptiness
too many stories
twelve stones
are striking the clock face
twelve swans
are flying away from winter

while night's stone
depicts rays of light
blind chimes
cry out for the absent ones

upon entering the room
you notice the flame
left behind when the fool
entered winter

旅行

那影子在飲水
那笑聲模仿
撐開黎明的光線的
崩潰方式

帶着書去旅行
書因旅行獲得年齡
因旅行而匿名
那深入佈景的馬
回首

你剛好到達
那人出生的地方

魚從水下看城市
水下有新鮮的誘餌
令人難堪的錨

TRAVEL

Shadow is drinking water
laughter is imitating
the way the collapse of light
opens up the dawn

the books one travels with
age because of the journey
become anonymous because of the journey
the horse pushing into the stage scenery
looks back

you have just arrived at
that person's place of birth

fish look up at the city from under water
there is fresh bait down there
an unbearable anchor

APPENDIX

Translating Bei Dao's "Untitled":
A Hundred Thousand Windows Shimmer

LK to CE, July 29, 2009 3:35 PM:

Here's the next BD poem, "Untitled."

I found it very difficult, which you'll be able to tell from my footnotes. One thing that comes to mind is that the first Chinese poet to write "Untitled" poems was Li Shangyin (ca. 813-858) of the late Tang. They're known for being dense, allusive, and hermetic, and are assumed to be allegorical, though no one knows for what, and also for being about love, though guesses about with whom proliferate. And it's not that they're untitled, but rather that their title—which was an important indicator of context and social referent in Chinese poetry up to that point—was the deliberately vague "Untitled." I imagine that Bei Dao may likely be invoking Li Shangyin in this and the other "Untitled" poems in *The Landscape Above Zero Degrees*.

Here's a quick bibliography for Li Shangyin in English, if you're interested:

- C. Graham, *Poems of the Late T'ang* (Penguin, 1965), pp. 141-173.
- James Liu, *The Poetry of Li Shang-yin: Ninth-Century Baroque Chinese Poet* (U. of Chicago, 1969)
- David Hinton, *Classical Chinese Poetry: An Anthology* (FSG, 2008), pp. 308-320
- Lucas Klein, a few Li Shangyin poems, *Fascicle 1* (www.fascicle.com; link seems to be dead, unfortunately)
- Robert Kelly's "Reading Li Shang-yin: Falling Flowers," in *Red Actions* (Black Sparrow, 1995), pp. 330-336

It's a goal of mine to translate the collected works of Li Shang-yin into English. I'd like the book to be called *Untitled*.

*

北島 《無題》	Bei Dao, "Untitled"
千百個窗戶閃爍	a hundred thousand windows shimmer[1]
這些預言者	these sooth-sayers[2]
在昨天與大海之間	between yesterday and the sea[3]
哦迷途的歡樂	murmur an errant delight[4]
橋成為現實	the bridge becomes reality
跨越公共的光線	stretching over a public[5] ray of light
而涉及昨日玫瑰的	and touching on yesterday's rose's
秘密旅行提供	secret voyage to provide[6]
一張紙一種困境	one sheet of paper one kind of dilemma[7]
母親的淚我的黎明	mother's tears my dawn[8]

[1] I like "shimmer" better than DH's "glimmer" because the word uses repeated /sh/ sounds (shǎnshuò), but another definition for the word is to be vague or evasive, maybe like "hem

and haw." Also, I don't think the number—which is actually more like "millions and millions"—should be taken literally. It strikes me that the number itself is a kind of shǎnshuò, or imprecise speech.

[2] I think I like "sooth-sayer" here better than "prophet" because the Chinese word includes the character for "speech."

[3] Probably in English these lines should be transposed, so that "between yesterday and the sea / these soothsayers..."

[4] For DH this line reads "o that joy of losing the way," which is considerably different from how I understand it. I read the line as é mítú de huānlè, where é = "v.: recite softly," mítú = "adj.: lose one's way; wrong path," and huānlè = "n.: joy, delight" (so that mítú de huānlè = "a lost joy, an errant delight"). For DH, it's ò mítú de huānlè, where ò = "oh, ah," and mítú de hu ānlè = "the joy of getting lost." Both are possible, but I'm sticking with my reading. At some point, though, we might want to ask Bei Dao, and see if he didn't mean to cover both meanings at once. If that's the case, we might have to figure out a way to encapsulate both meanings in their simultaneity in English.

[5] DH has this as "the public," but I don't think gōnggòng can be a noun, only an adjective.

[6] The grammar of this poem is particularly complicated, and I find myself reading it differently from Hinton at just about each turn. I'll exchange line breaks for punctuation to show the different readings. Hinton: "A bridge becomes reality, spanning the public's gleam, and the clandestine journey involving yesterday's rose offers a sheet of paper, a dilemma." Me: "The bridge becomes reality stretching over a public ray of light and touching on yesterday's rose's secret voyage to provide a certain dilemma for every sheet of paper." I guess we just have to pick whichever one we like better.

[7] My English here is admittedly strange, and strained. I think it probably means, as would be colloquial Chinese, "a kind of dilemma per sheet of paper" (kind of like how we say "one man, one vote"). See above.

[8] The implied grammar here is probably parallel to the line above, so that, if "one piece of paper one kind of dilemma" means "a kind of dilemma for each sheet of paper," then this probably means "a dawn for me for each of mother's tears."

*

CE to LK, July 29, 2009, 4:02 PM:

Yes, a complicated one. But your information in your notes is very useful.

> [UNTITLED]
>
> Millions of windows shimmer
> between yesterday and the sea
> these sooth-sayers
> murmur an errant delight
>
> The bridge becomes reality
> spanning a public ray of light
> and touching on the secret voyage of
> yesterday's rose providing
> a certain dilemma for each sheet of paper
>
> for me a dawn for each of my mother's tears

Try this version and let me know where I have missed a point.

[CE then revises this version and sends a new one to LK later the same day:]

[UNTITLED]

A hundred thousand windows shimmer
between yesterday and the sea
these sooth-sayers
recite lost joys

A bridge becomes reality
spanning public rays of light,
touching on the secret voyage of
yesterday's rose providing
for each sheet of paper a certain dilemma

for each of my dawns my mother's tears

*

LK to CE, July 30, 2009, 11:07 AM:

I think this is good. See attached comments. My only worry
is that we're doing too much to lock the poem down to one
meaning, as opposed to leaving it open to the ambiguities that
would lead to David Hinton's translation.

UNTITLED

A hundred thousand windows [shimmer]
between yesterday and the sea
these sooth-sayers
[recite] lost joys

A bridge becomes reality
spanning public rays of light,
[touching on] the secret voyage of
yesterday's rose providing
for each sheet of paper a certain dilemma

[for each of my dawns my mother's tears]

COMMENT: I'm trying to think of a word
that would go with "shimmer" to suggest
a kind of verbal beating-around-the-bush.
How about "shimmer and shuffle"?

COMMENT: "recite" is good, but the verb
in Chinese suggests low tones. "intone"?
something else?

COMMENT: The Ch. word for "touching
on" is explicitly verbal, e.g., "your argu-
ment touches on the issue that..." Is this
clear in the English?

COMMENT: I guess it's the same, but I
think the Ch. says, "one of my dawns
for each mother's tear." Of course, then
we get into questions about whether it's
each mother's tear, or mothers' tear, or
tears, or...

120

*

CE to LK, July 30, 2009, 2:27 PM:

Another version. "Shimmer and shuffle" seem definitely off
to me.

The only way I can see using "shuffle" is to replace "in-
tone" with it.

I think it would be ok to create an extra half line with "pro-
viding," to keep the prosody in balance.

The last two lines are now parallel. Do they pretty much
match the Chinese?

To think of the bridge itself "touching on" is a little unreal.
Thus "bordering on" which I think is a little more indirect and
mysterious, the bridge itself being a kind of border.

You imply that we are making the poem too logical. Can
you point out where?

[UNTITLED]

A hundred thousand windows shimmer
between yesterday and the sea
these sooth-sayers
intone errant delights

A bridge becomes reality
spanning public rays of light
and bordering on the secret voyage of
yesterday's rose
                    providing
one kind of dilemma for each sheet of paper

one of my dawns for each mother's tears

*

121

LK to CE, August 2, 2009, 12:00 PM:

Sorry for the delay. Had to consider a number of things with this poem (mostly, does my reading of the poem do more than fulfill the poem the way I want it to be, or does it respond to what the poem says?), & of course the rest of life gets in the way sometimes. Anyway, here are my comments, attached:

UNTITLED

A hundred thousand windows shimmer
between yesterday and the sea
these sooth-sayers
[intone errant delights]

COMMENT: I asked my wife about this poem, & she says that this line is probably closer to Hinton's reading. So, "oh, the joy in getting lost." That would also mean that we wouldn't need to transpose lines 2 and 3.

A bridge becomes reality
spanning public rays of light
and bordering on the secret voyage of
yesterday's rose
                [providing]
one [kind of] dilemma for each sheet of paper

one of my dawns for each of my mother's tears

COMMENT: I like this, but since BD doesn't do it, I'm a bit hesitant to write it this way.
COMMENT: This might be superfluous. What do you think?

As you can see, I asked my wife about the poem, & she doesn't agree with my reading of the first stanza, so I think we should move closer to Hinton's stanza 1, at least in terms of understanding. Also, the word we now have as "shimmer" is, pretty much, just "shimmer." The verbal obfuscation I felt implicit in the word is only there to the extent that "beating" implies "beating around the bush"; as in, not that much, really.

I think "bordering on" is fine. It's more literal as "touching on," but I like your reading of it, a bridge as something that crosses borders and becomes a border.

We're good with the last two lines, I think.

Finally, nice to have BD's take on what he'd like translated. FN#1

*

CE to LK, August 2, 2009, 12:24 PM:

Dear Lucas:

Your letter: I don't understand the main point you are making in paragraph 2. What is wrong with "shimmer"? What is the sense of the word that we must try to match?

I don't like repeating what Hinton has done in stanza one. I can't believe that his translation is absolutely accurate.

Once you give me more information on the shimmer problem, and explain, please, the difference between the way you and your wife now read stanza 1 AND what Hinton has, then I can do another draft of the poem.

*

LK to CE, August 2, 2009, 1:07 PM:

Hi, Clayton—

My point, in para. 2 was that nothing's wrong with "shimmer." The word is *"shanshuo,"* which means "shimmer, flicker," but is also part of a phrase *"shanshuo qi ci,"* which literally means "shimmer your words" and means "to vacillate." I felt like *"shanshuo"* ("shimmer") implied *"shanshuo qi ci"* ("to vacillate"), and so I was looking for a word that would encompass both in English. But now I think that we don't need to do that, and that "shimmer" is good enough.

Also, it comes down to the "e" or "o" problem in line 4. I had read it as "e" (to intone), but I guess that would be a very obscure reading of the word. That doesn't mean it isn't so, but it does mean that most people reading the poem are going to see it meaning, "oh, ah."

I also don't like what Hinton has done with stanza one. I prefer the version we had based on my first reading. But that doesn't mean that that's what BD meant for it to say. Now, it's our translation, so we can do what we want, or we could also ask BD which version he prefers.

*

CE to LK, August 2, 2009, 3:15 PM:

I am now rethinking our Introduction and realize that one useful thing we could do would be to print all the versions of a single poem, with the Chinese and your right-hand box commentaries. That way no one would be puzzled as to our procedure.

In the first stanza, I am getting, now, the impression that the windows are the sooth-sayers, and that the whole first stanza is variations on what they evoke. They are the sooth-sayers either murmuring/reciting/or intoning whatever. Something in me wants to read the first stanza this way (I know it is incorrect):

> A hundred thousand windows vacillate
> between yesterday and the sea
> sooth-sayers shimmering with
> errant delights

Which leads quite naturally then to

> A bridge becomes reality
> spanning public rays of light
> and bordering on the secret voyage of
> yesterday's rose provoking
> one dilemma for each sheet of paper
>
> one dawn for each of my mother's tears

I know "provoke" and "shimmering" are off, but they make for a very interesting poem! Alas...

*

LK to CE, August 4, 2009, 12:20 PM:

I really like your response to the BD poem as it stands. You're right that it involves some inaccuracies, but knowing that it's coming from you, I think it's great. That said, I've asked another native Chinese speaker about my reading of the poem, and since she came back with something closer to David Hinton's understanding, I've gone back for another version, incorporating some of where we've gotten already. Please let me know if you see any improvements.

> [UNTITLED]
>
> A hundred thousand windows waver
> these sooth-sayers
> between yesterday and the sea
> oh joy astray
>
> a bridge becomes reality
> spanning public rays of light
> while the secret voyage touching
> yesterday's rose provides
> a dilemma for each piece of paper
>
> my dawn for each of mother's tears

*

CE to LK, August 4, 2009, 2:34 PM:

Dear Lucas,
I think you understand that I did not intend my last somewhat capricious version of "Untitled" as our version.

As for your new one: I like both "shimmer" and "vacillate" better than "waver." I dislike the w w play, which is flat-footed as I hear it, and I think the word is weaker than either of the earlier two.

I also think that in English the reversal of lines 2 and 3 is very effective. Putting "these sooth-sayers" after "windows waver" seems to change the subject.

Alas, I really dislike "oh joy astray." To my ear it is on the same level as "O bird thou never wer't" (by Shelley). It is old-fashioned "poetic."

Also your new version loses the implicit "logic of metaphor" in the first four lines. Your initial fourth line is much more engaging than the current one. I gather you now do not feel that "murmur" (or intone) "an errant delight" is correct?

The second stanza is ok, except that I thought the last two lines were parallel (initially: "a kind of dilemma for..." "a dawn for..." and you initially had "my" before "mother" which makes the ending personally acute, if somewhat sentimental. Without the "my" I think we have sentimentality without personal acuteness.

I guess I should wait to do another version. If you have decided that "oh joy astray" is an accurate translation for the Chinese, well, I guess we will have to keep it... Actually, Hinton's "oh the joy of losing the way" is better.

*

LK to CE, August 4, 2009, 5:03 PM:

Hi, Clayton—

What I liked about "waver" was that I thought it got at both "shimmer" and "vacillate," though Chinese readers have told me that they think I'm going too far with reading "vacillate" into "shimmer." So we stay with "shimmer."

With "oh joy astray" I was trying to get at something that could mean both "the joy you feel when astray" and "joy that is itself astray." Not liking the phrase, we'll have to choose ("the joy you feel when astray" is what most Chinese readers are going to understand from those lines), but I'm afraid the reason you don't like it—and why I wish I could trust my desire for it to be "murmur/intone"—is because of the "oh." Do you see any way around it?

I think the problem now is the first stanza. We seem all right at least with the meaning of the second.

*

CE to LK, August 5, 2009, 2:34 PM:

The first stanza would read better if set in three lines (lines 3 and 4 as one line). But I suppose you would not feel this would effectively translate the original.

The lines in the second stanza could be presented more forcefully if set in four and not in five lines.

*

LK to CE, August 5, 2009, 4:06 PM:

Hi, Clayton—

I think we have a sense of how the poem works based on my first reading (intoning errant delights, etc). I think we need to have a sense of how the poem would work based on my second reading, which is close to Hinton's reading, and which a couple of poetry-reading Chinese friends of mine have convinced me is the way they read the poem.

I see stanza one as saying:

127

> A hundred thousand windows shimmer
> these sooth-sayers
> are between yesterday and the sea
> oh the joys of getting lost

That is, "A hundred thousand windows [sooth-sayers] shimmer. These sooth-sayers are [lost] between yesterday and the sea. Oh, the joy of getting lost." It's unclear to me whether your idea to transpose the lines, so that "windows shimmer between yesterday and the sea" gets us as close to the Chinese as possible, or it if changes the logic of Bei Dao's stanza. I do, at any rate, think that "intone" is a misreading. Unfortunately, it's one of those misreadings that make the poem more interesting.

Second stanza:

> A bridge becomes reality
> spanning public rays of light
> while the secret voyage touching
> yesterday's rose provides
> a dilemma for each sheet of paper

That is, "A bridge, spanning public rays of light, becomes reality, while the secret voyage that touches on the rose of yesterday provides a dilemma for each sheet of paper." I'm not sure what this image means, but I think we are dealing with a contrast here between "public" and "secret," between the bridge and the voyage. Without the preposition "while" or its equivalent, I think the contrast gets lost in favor of a suggestion (as per stanza one, where we believe that windows = sooth-sayers) that the bridge is the secret voyage.

This may be the dilemma we have on this blank page of ours.

I'm fine with changing the line breaks if we think it's necessary.

*

CE to LK, August 5, 2009, 4:08 PM

Like this? I don't think we need to revise breaks and line lengths. We would be asking for criticism, and the gain I now think is not worth it.

> [UNTITLED]
>
> A hundred thousand windows shimmer
> these sooth-sayers
> are between yesterday and the sea
> O the joys of getting lost
>
> A bridge becomes reality
> spanning public rays of light
> while the secret voyage touching
> yesterday's rose provides
> a dilemma for each sheet of paper
>
> my dawn for each of my mother's tears

*

LK to CE, August 5, 2009, 5:17 PM:

I do like it, and think it does what Bei Dao wanted it to do (as I understand from my reading of the Chinese). And I think presenting some of our stops on the way to our final understanding in an introduction would be a great way to explain our process, and the requirements of translation.

Two questions: in the last line, do you think we need to specify "my dawn" for each of my mother's tears?

Also, what if in line four, instead of "Oh the joys of getting lost," we said, "Oh joy getting lost." I think it has an ambiguity that echoes BD's original.

*

CE to LK, August 5, 2009, 5:33 PM:

On second thought: I think the repetition of "my" in the last line is less effective than leaving it as it is. The reader understands that the sheet of paper evokes the paper on which a poem is written, thus the consciousness of the piece is clearly at that point in Bei Dao's court. If so, and if it is his mother's tears in the last line, then the dawn is one he implicitly experiences too. Plus we have a nice parallel (which you earlier supported, I think)   a dilemma   a dawn

my dawn   also sounds rather overly possessive to me.

What do you think?

*

LK to CE, August 5, 2009, 5:40 PM:

Agreed. I think that it's implicitly clear that if we're talking about my mother, we're talking about my dawn.

***

NOTE

On August 2, 2009, Bei Dao sent the following letter to Clayton:

Dear Clayton:

How have you been? Today is my birthday of 60. I will be leaving for Paris tomorrow and will be back to Hong Kong on August 25.

Here is the list of poems can be translated if you like:

Beyond
Apple and Brute Stone
New Century
Asking the Sky
A Portrait
On Eternity
Background
Untitled (in the plains of a father's imagination)
This Day
February
We
Bright Mirror
Nightwatch
Wax
Untitled (in waking there is freedom)
Winter Travels
Journey

BEI DAO, born in Beijing in 1949, has lived in more than six countries and has taught and lectured around the world. He has received numerous international awards for his poetry, and is an honorary member of The American Academy of Arts and Letters. Now a US citizen, Bei Dao is professor of Humanities in the Center for East Asian Studies at the Chinese University of Hong Kong. His new and selected poetry was published as *The Rose of Time* by New Directions in 2010.

CLAYTON ESHLEMAN's recent publications include *The Complete Poetry of César Vallejo* (University of California Press, 2007), *Archaic Design* (Black Widow Press, 2007), *The Grindstone of Rapport* (BWP, 2008), *Anticline* (BWP, 2010), and a translation of Bernard Bador's *Curdled Skulls* (BWP, 2011). This spring Wesleyan University Press will bring out his cotranslation with A. James Arnold of Aimé Césaire's *Solar Throat Slashed*. He has recently completed a 35-page poem entitled "An Anatomy of the Night," as well as a translation of "Sakra Boccata" by José Antonio Mazzotti.

LUCAS KLEIN—a former radio DJ and union organizer—is a writer, translator, and editor of *CipherJournal.com*. His translations, essays, and poems have appeared or are forthcoming at *Two Lines*, *Jacket*, and *Drunken Boat*, and he regularly reviews books for *Rain Taxi* and other venues. A graduate of Middlebury College (BA) and Yale University (PhD), he is Assistant Professor in the department of Chinese, Translation & Linguistics at City University of Hong Kong, and is at work on translations of Tang dynasty poet Li Shangyin and contemporary poet Xi Chuan.

TITLES FROM BLACK WIDOW PRESS

TRANSLATION SERIES

Approximate Man and Other Writings
by Tristan Tzara. Translated and edited
by Mary Ann Caws.

Art Poétique by Guillevic.
Translated by Maureen Smith.

The Big Game
by Benjamin Péret. Translated with an
introduction by Marilyn Kallet.

Capital of Pain by Paul Eluard.
Translated by Mary Ann Caws, Patricia Terry,
and Nancy Kline.

Chanson Dada: Selected Poems by Tristan Tzara.
Translated with an introduction and essay by
Lee Harwood.

*Essential Poems and Writings of Joyce Mansour: A
Bilingual Anthology*
Translated with an introduction by
Serge Gavronsky.

Essential Poems and Prose of Jules Laforgue
Translated and edited by Patricia Terry.

*Essential Poems and Writings of
Robert Desnos: A Bilingual Anthology*
Edited with an introduction and essay
by Mary Ann Caws.

EyeSeas (Les Ziaux) by Raymond Queneau.
Translated with an introduction by Daniela
Hurezanu and Stephen Kessler.

Furor and Mystery & Other Writings
by René Char. Edited and translated by
Mary Ann Caws and Nancy Kline.

The Inventor of Love & Other Writings
by Gherasim Luca. Translated by Julian
and Laura Semilian. Introduction by
Andrei Codrescu. Essay by Petre Răileanu.

La Fontaine's Bawdy by Jean de la Fontaine.
Translated with an introduction by
Norman R. Shapiro.

Last Love Poems of Paul Eluard
Translated with an introduction by
Marilyn Kallet.

Love, Poetry (L'amour la poésie)
by Paul Eluard. Translated with an essay
by Stuart Kendall.

Poems of André Breton: A Bilingual Anthology
Translated with essays by Jean-Pierre
Cauvin and Mary Ann Caws.

Poems of A.O. Barnabooth by Valéry Larbaud.
Translated by Ron Padgett and Bill Zavatsky.

Preversities: A Jacques Prévert Sampler
Translated and edited by Norman R. Shapiro.

The Sea and Other Poems by Guillevic.
Translated by Patricia Terry. Introduction by
Monique Chefdor.

To Speak, to Tell You? Poems by Sabine Sicaud.
Translated by Norman R. Shapiro. Introduc-
tion and notes by Odile Ayral-Clause.

FORTHCOMING TRANSLATIONS

Essential Poems and Writings of Pierre Reverdy
Translated by Mary Ann Caws and
Patricia Terry.

A Life of Poems, Poems of a Life by Anna de
Noailles. Translated by Norman R. Shapiro.
Introduction by Catherine Perry.

MODERN POETRY SERIES

An Alchemist with One Eye on Fire
by Clayton Eshleman

Anticline by Clayton Eshleman

Archaic Design by Clayton Eshleman

Backscatter: New and Selected Poems
by John Olson

The Caveat Onus by Dave Brinks.
The complete cycle, four volumes in one.

Concealments and Caprichos
by Jerome Rothenberg

Crusader-Woman by Ruxandra Cesereanu.
Translated by Adam J. Sorkin. Introduction
by Andrei Codrescu.

Curdled Skulls: Poems of Bernard Bador
Translated by the author with Clayton
Eshleman.

Endure: Poems by Bei Dao
Translated by Clayton Eshleman and
Lucas Klein

Fire Exit by Robert Kelly

Forgiven Submarine
by Ruxandra Cesereanu and Andrei Codrescu

The Grindstone of Rapport:
A Clayton Eshleman Reader
Forty years of poetry, prose, and translations.

Packing Light: New and Selected Poems
by Marilyn Kallet

The Present Tense of the World:
Poems 2000–2009 by Amina Saïd.
Translated with an introduction by Marilyn
Hacker.

Signal from Draco: New and Selected Poems
by Mebane Robertson

FORTHCOMING

MODERN POETRY TITLES

City Without People: The Katrina Poems
Niyi Osundare

Exile is My Trade: A Habib Tengour Reader
Translated by Pierre Joris.

from stone this running by Heller Levinson

Larynx Galaxy by John Olson

Memory Wing by Bill Lavender

LITERARY THEORY / BIOGRAPHY SERIES

Revolution of the Mind:
The Life of André Breton
by Mark Polizzotti. Revised
and augmented edition.

WWW.BLACKWIDOWPRESS.COM